MW00442684

Earn More Tips on
Your Very Next Shift…
even if you're a bad waiter

Earn More Tips on
Your Very Next Shift…
even if you're a bad waiter

by
Steve DiGioia

Dedicated to my wife Madeline,
for enduring countless hours listening to the complaints and
frustrations from my many years as a hospitality manager, and for
being the best wife I could have ever asked for…she's a pretty good
book editor as well.

And to the other two ladies in my life, my daughters Annmarie &
Christine. I could never ask for more joy.

Contents

Why Did I Write This Book? 1

Why Should I Care If You Earn More Tips? 5

What I Will Not Teach You. 7

Magical Table Greeting. 9

Two Minutes or Two Bites. 15

Smile… I Know You Can Do It. 19

So What Do You Recommend? 21

Is There Anything Else I May Get For You? 25

Get That Kid His Mac & Cheese First. 27

I'm a Waiter, Not a Salesman. 29

Happy Birthday To You. 33

I Have My Own Stuff To Talk About. 35

Know Thy Substitutions. 39

Where Did I Leave That Thing? 43

My Busboy, My Partner. 47

Where's The Nearest Bookstore? 51

Do They Really Need To Ask For It? 55

Now Get Outta My Way? 61

Take My Picture, Please. 65

Sell The Wine Everytime. 67

Goodnight My Guest. 71

Why Do I Keep Referring To The Customer As Guest? 75

Do I Really Care About My Guest? 77

It's a Win Win Situation. 79

Why Did I Write This Book?

Over the years I've known many waiters; most have had only one thing in mind...to earn more tips! They usually couldn't give a damn about the restaurant or company they worked for, just about their own pocket.

These waiters came in every possible variety; the hardworking, studious college kid that was very driven and worked 6-days a week to put himself through school; the gravelly-voiced divorced mom of 4 grown kids that needed to pay her bills and get her life back on track; the "hot" chick that thought her looks, and boobs, was her ticket to fame and fortune and that being a waiter was only a temporary setback for her; and the overweight nerdy-guy that really couldn't relate well with his customers, continually came in late and never got a close shave but always found time to play dungeons & dragons.

They all had one thing in common, they wanted to earn as much in tips on each shift as they possibly could! And why not?

The college kid had textbooks that cost over $100 each and dad didn't have the finances to pay for his college architect classes. The gravelly-voiced mom was still smoking 2 packs of cigarettes a day, buying her tabloid magazines and trying to make the rent each month.

The hot chick was always hanging out in the newest and trendiest bars and clubs hoping to be spotted by some celebrity or talent scout, so she needed to be dressed in all the top designed duds.

The overweight nerdy-guy, well I didn't know what the heck he really needed the money for. I guess those video games and cheese puffs are getting too expensive.

Either way their main focus was on their needs in the short term, never on the long term. They never thought of what they could do differently today to make their tomorrow better. And, of course, they couldn't care about the long term success of the restaurant either.

They didn't realize that if they took more than just a passing interest in being a better waiter, or bartender, that they will get to their REAL goal faster. **The goal of earning more tips**.

Note: During this book I will usually refer only to waiters since this is my main focus but much of the information I will give you will just as easily pertain to a bartender, as well, and a hostess; a busboy; a food runner. You get the idea.

So after many years as a manager in the hospitality business, constantly teaching the company's S.O.P.'s to the new recruits, dolling out disciplinary forms, making sure you set the silverware correctly, checking your salt and pepper shakers and covering your butt when you screw-up or call out sick at the last minute, I thought I will finally look at things from the waiter's point of view.

How can you make more money in tips right away, and even on your very next shift?

Question: So what's the main motive of a waiter?

Answer: Move them in and out and hope I get a good tip. But I'm not gonna work too hard for that.

If I were a waiter, why would I care about the company's payroll? Why should I care about the chef's food cost? How am I supposed to remember all the specials we have today? And don't even tell me that the newest hotshot manager wants to shrink my section from 6 tables down to 3. Of course I will get pissed off, how am I supposed to make money with only 3 tables?

But you see I'm a little sneaky, I have my own motive as well. I think I can kill two birds with one stone as they say. I think I've come up with a few sure-fire ways that any waiter can earn more tips, even if they are a bad waiter...and still take care of the interests of the company as well.

...but why should I care if you earn more tips?

Why Should I Care if You Earn More Tips?

Good question. As a manager of a hotel or restaurant, we don't pay your tips, the customer does. We pay you a small hourly wage and you keep the tips you earn. If you get stiffed that's not my problem, it's yours.

The law in most states is that you as the server must pay the tax on the tips you receive and are **expected** to receive, whether you get stiffed or not. In many states, the restaurant will make you pay the tax on tips you didn't receive, based on your total sales, and will even deduct it from your check.

So I do have certain paperwork I need to do to track all of this, but whether you get a 20% cash tip or 15% put on the check when the customer paid by credit card it is not my concern.

Depending where in the country you work, the hourly rate of an a la carte waiter will vary greatly from as little as $2.00 per hour to maybe a little over $4.00. This is because our "all-caring" government allows a business that employs "tipped personnel" to be paid less than the federal minimum wage. There's much more that goes into this but since I'm not versed in tax-law mumbo jumbo, I'll leave that discussion to the experts.

So regardless, it's in your best interest as a waiter to earn more tips. So how do you do this?

And why should I care?

> **I care because a waiter that is making a good living is usually a happy employee.**

Happy employees usually do a better job. Employees that do a better job allow the business to be more successful. Businesses that are more successful make more money, have a longer profitable business cycle and usually pay managers like me more money as well.

So it's a win-win situation for all. You as the waiter get to make lasting memories for the customers that walk in our doors and we all get paid.

You as a waiter get to line your pockets with cash and the business sees repeat guests. Repeat guests that bring in their friends and family to eat and drink here too.

We see our profits go up and take more money to the bank. This allows us to hire more people, make long-range plans for expansion, large equipment purchases or for whatever the business needs.

You as a waiter really couldn't care about that stuff but at least you got paid!

So, since the title of this book is "Earning More Tips on Your Very Next Shift", how do you do this? Even if you're a bad waiter?

You see, I have a lot of faith in you, I know you can do this.

You just need a few basic skills, skills that are easy to learn. Skills, tips, tricks, whatever you want to call them, they can be used on your very next shift.

And you WILL earn more tips if you use them.

...but what will I not teach you?

6

What I Will Not Teach You

During my research to prepare for writing this book, I scoured the internet for information that was already written by others on this topic. I wanted to see what the competition was up to. I was amazed by what I found.

Some of the recommendations were so bad that I had to stop looking. Did ANY of these people ever actually work as a waiter or manage a restaurant? If so, they probably were not very successful.

Here is a brief listing of some things I found that were supposed to help a waiter earn more tips.

- Write your name and a smiley face on the check
- Give a piece of candy to the customer with the check
- Bend or crouch down on the side of the table when speaking with the guest
- Lightly touch the customer sometime during their meal
- Wear a red shirt, red lipstick or a flower in your hair (for the ladies)
- Carry more than one pen

Are they kidding? I can't tell you how many blogs, articles and other web sites mentioned some of the same things. I think they all copied each other's dumb ideas. And yes, dumb they are.

These ideas are embarrassing and childish. Give a piece of candy when you present the check to the guest. What are we in preschool?

Write a smiley face on the check? You might just get stiffed now because of that.

Carry more than one pen? Well, that's a no-brainer but it won't make you any more money.

Bend or crouch down while taking the order? Now you're getting in my face. Please don't do that.

Lightly touch me…not unless you want a fat lip!

> **These are childish, improper and useless things to tell a waiter, especially one that is young and inexperienced and just trying to learn more about their trade.**

This will do nothing more than to instill bad habits that will be difficult to break out of.

You are a professional. You take pride in your job, your profession. You do not need to resort to worthless tactics and I won't insult you with stuff like this.

So I stopped looking. I don't need anyone's help to write this book, surely not from any of those "experts". I have been in this business, in one manner or another, for 25+ years and have seen some of the best and worst at their trade. And I learned from all of them. The good and the bad. I learned what REALLY works!

Now I will share it with you.

…on with your training.

Magical Table Greeting

Your first customer service tip is the single most important piece of information that I can ever give you. Not just so you can make more tip money but for life as well.

When you open your arms, your heart and soul and let your defenses down for a moment, just one moment, and greet your customer with a warm sincere smile, they will know that you care about them. That you care enough to make sure they are taken care of.

~~~~~~~~~~~~~~~~~~~~~~~~~~

Here's the scenario:

Three (3) waiters are working on tonight's shift at the restaurant. Each is a long-standing employee with many years of service and experience. Each waiter knows the entire menu and has a decent operational knowledge of wine.

Three equally talented waiters but with very different approaches when they greet their guests. See which table-side greeting you think is best.

Waiter #1

"Hi guys, how are you today? What can I get you guys to drink?" After the waiter takes their drink orders he/she finishes with "Ok guys, I'll be right back."

<u>Waiter #2</u>

(Waiter looking down at notepad and speaking softly) "Hi, I'm Steve. Can I start you off with a drink from the bar or are you ready to order?"

<u>Waiter #3</u>

"Good evening, welcome. Welcome to the _____ Restaurant. My name is Steve and I will be your server tonight."

"I just wanted you to know that you will have a GREAT meal tonight and it's MY job to make sure you're well taken care of. So if there's anything you need while you are here, please let me know."

"Have you decided on your dinner choices yet or may I get you a drink from our fantastic bartender first?"

~~~~~~~~~~~~~~~~~~~~~~~~~~~~

Which of these three servers do you think will provide better customer service?

Which of these servers would you prefer taking care of you if you were a guest in this restaurant?

Which of these servers do you think earns more in tips?

If you're like most people you will answer each question with waiter #3, but why?

Remember that I said all three of these waiters had the exact same experience and knowledge? Then why did you pick #3? If you didn't pick #3 then it's time to get out of the business!

What makes this a magical table greeting is that the waiter has a great MINDSET.

A mindset of service, a culture of service. One that focuses on the guest satisfaction first, then the waiters tasks at hand second.

The guest now knows what to expect from his waiter. His enjoyment and satisfaction is the waiter's primary concern and is his **JOB** to take care of you.

> ### I bet that customer is already reaching for his wallet to get the waiter's big tip ready! That tip should be yours.

Waiter #3 immediately has put the guests at ease and made them feel welcome. Ah, the warmest word in the English language, welcome.

In the first two table-side greetings I gave you, do you think the server's main focus was on the guest's happiness, or their enjoyment of the evening? Of course not.

Waiter #1 kept referring to his guests as "guys". What if this was a table of women? I don't think that if your mom was out to lunch with a few of her friends she would like to be called a guy!

There is never a reason to refer to a person's gender or age. So don't do it.

Waiter #2 was either too shy or didn't care enough to even look at his guests in the eye. And he spoke too softly as well.

If you can't relate in a pleasant professional manner with people that want to give you their money, then maybe this business is not for you.

Too many people that are in the position to "greet" people never actually do that. They may say hi or hello but that is nothing more than an acknowledgement that someone has entered your space. That's it!

When you "welcome" someone you are allowing them full access to "your space", to treat your space as if it was "their space", their home.

Remember, that's the reason why we go out to eat. Not just to fill our stomachs, but to be taken care of. We can get food anywhere but why do we go to a specific restaurant? Or a specific business, regardless of what type it is?

Because we feel good when we go there. Because of how they make us feel welcome. Because they make us feel special.

If you don't feel special why keep going back?

Good question. Now let's try this...

~~~~~~~~~~~~~~~~~~~~~~~~~~

Here's another scenario:

Restaurant #1

> Has great food but terrible service. Service that makes you feel as if you weren't appreciated, or it didn't matter if you spent your money there or not? Wait staff that never checked back with you during the meal; silverware that was spotty; food that was usually prepared wrong and not the way you wanted.

Restaurant #2

> Has average food but the hostess and manager knew your name, greeted you as if you were family, and even remembered the table you liked or the specific drink you always requested. The waiter was always very attentive, you never had to ask for your beverage to be refilled and he proudly stated that his main focus was that you had a great evening.

~~~~~~~~~~~~~~~~~~~~~~~~

Which restaurant would you want to go back to time and time again?

Which restaurant would you recommend to your friends?

Which restaurant DESERVES your business?

The answer is Restaurant #2.

So what is different in these 2 examples? SERVICE.

It starts with a mindset that you will take care of every guest that walks into the door as if they are your family and has just come to your house for a holiday dinner. If that was the case would you ever let them feel unwanted or unappreciated? Made to feel that you didn't care if they left happy or not?

Would you ever treat your grandma that way? Of course you wouldn't. So don't treat your guests that way either.

Oh, another question or two:

Which of these two restaurants do you think is busier and makes more money?

Which restaurant would you want to work in?

In which restaurant do you think the waiters make bigger tips?

Now that you have my Magical Table Greeting you can make more money for yourself and for your restaurant as well…

…but after their food is served, make sure you check back with your guest.

Two Minutes or Two Bites

Too many restaurants today rely on food runners to deliver the guest's food. This is sad. Sad because on average your waiter doesn't even know that your food was delivered to your table.

This is especially the case in many of this country's theme restaurants. They're more interested in churning the customers in and out then to make sure their experience is the best it could be when they are there. The waiter takes the order, the food runner delivers the food, the waiter comes back and drops the check.

But what if the food is not to your liking? What if the food runner forgot your side order of asparagus? What if the burger came out with steak fries instead of the shoe-string fries as you asked? What if the steak was undercooked? Your waiter will never know since someone else delivered your food.

Now as a hungry customer you cut into your steak and see that your medium-well steak came to you as a medium-rare. Too pink for your taste. Ok, not a major problem but something you need to deal with. You'll just tell your waiter that your steak is under cooked and ask for it to be cooked a little more.

But you can't, your waiter is nowhere to be found. Now passing moments seem like minutes. Minutes seem like hours and still no waiter. Your fellow diners have either almost finished their meal or have stopped eating in sympathy for you. They're too polite to keep eating. Nice folks you have with you.

So even if your waiter used the "Magical Table Greeting" who cares? Not you. You're the customer and you have a steak that you can't eat and you can't find the damn waiter to get it fixed.

The cardinal rule in this business is:

Check back on your guest in two minutes or two bites.

You, as a waiter, just took a wonderful dining experience and ruined it because you couldn't find the time to check back on your customer! Why would you do that?

Put yourself in that guest's shoes. Do you want to have to hunt around to find your waiter just so you can get something to eat? I don't think so.

Would you give that waiter a big tip? Probably not.

So now comes the excuses from the waiter:

- I was taking care of another table

- My manager was asking me a question

- I was in the kitchen checking on my food

As a manager, my answers to these excuses are:

- The guest that is waiting for you to grace their table with a visit so he can tell you about your steak is not concerned about the other table. He just wants you to pay attention to him.

- Maybe the manager was really asking you why your customer is looking around the room and finally found a busboy to ask him to find his waiter; YOU!

- What good was done by you being in the kitchen checking on "your" food? You sure didn't check on the food that was just delivered to your table.

Oh, you DIDN'T check on the food that was delivered to your table? But you want a big tip.

You found many excuses to offer in your defense for not checking on your guest…but you want a big tip.

The guest's satisfaction was not your primary concern…but you want a big tip.

Do you see a pattern here? I'm not picking on you as a waiter. I just want you to pay more attention to the needs of the guest first. I just want you to check back with the guest within two minutes or two bites to see if they are happy with their meal. If they are not happy you can address it right away. Don't let your guest wait.

Ultimately the guest gets what he wants and you know they are taken care of. If you take care of the guest, they will take care of you. If not, don't expect much from them.

…especially if you didn't smile.

Smile…I Know You Can Do It

You've experienced it. You come into work with a real big smile on your face and suddenly people respond to you with a smile of their own and seem to treat you better.

It's a well-researched social phenomenon. In fact, just looking at photos of happy-faced people has been shown to make a person's brain waves go into a happier mode.

When someone smiles, they are exhibiting positive emotions. Those positive emotions can affect the way a person acts and feels. Since the body and mind work so closely together, it is only natural that those positive feelings will affect the body in a positive way.

So how does this relate to you as a waiter?

- Well maybe your guests will also respond to you in a positive manner.
- Maybe they will become a little more forgiving if their steak was not cooked EXACTLY the way they wanted or if their food was delayed.
- Maybe they will like your service more, or even think you are a better waiter.

Either way, if the research is correct, your positive emotions may rub off on your guests and their dining experience will be perceived to be more enjoyable. **Maybe you will even get a bigger tip!**

But what if you are having a bad day? What if things around you are falling apart? You just can't feel "positive" today. What if you are just miserable?

There's nothing worse than a miserable waiter. Now to be honest, I've never been taken care of by a miserable waiter nor have I had the misfortune of having one work for me. But we have all had a server or bartender that had something else on their mind. Something that prevented them from focusing on me, their guest. And that's understandable.

We don't live in a vacuum. We all have bills to pay, we all have problems to deal with. I remember many years ago when I had to put my cat to sleep. She was very sick and kept looking at me with her big brown eyes as she lay there taking her final breaths. When it was over I cried all the way to my car. And continued to cry as I drove to work. Yes work! I was in a real cranky mood for the entire day until I was able to go home and sleep it off.

Now imagine if I was a waiter. There was no way I would have been able to put on a happy face, let alone a big smile, on that day. But every guest at my tables would not have cared about my cat. Nor should they. They would have come in my restaurant with an empty belly and looking to get it filled. And to be served by a pleasant waiter, with a smile.

That's why so many "actors" are very good as a waiter or bartender. They are used to putting on a show even if they have other issues to deal with behind the scenes. They can smile, tell a story and even be a good listener if needed. You would never know their cat just died.

So please, take a word of advice from me. Be an actor. Put your personal issues aside. The guests don't care. But if you care about getting a big tip, make that smile show. No matter what.

…maybe you can recommend a good entrée to the guest as well.

So, What Do You Recommend?

Big Frankie comes into your restaurant. You know the type, big guy, hands like a baseball mitt, a loud voice and brags about almost everything. Big Frankie is always the star of the show and wants you to know it.

Tonight he comes in with a few of his buddies. It's show time…

You greet Frankie and his friends in a magical way and he calls you by your name. So far so good, hey Big Frankie seems like a cool guy. Frankie is trying to impress the boys so he wants to order for them all. When one of his buddies wasn't too crazy with what Frankie ordered he asks you "hey Steve, what do you recommend?"

First sign of trouble, but you've got this. You know just what to recommend to one of your new buddies. You make what seems to be a great suggestion, "I'm not that crazy with that dish either. I highly recommend the 32oz porterhouse steak. It melts in your mouth and is my favorite thing we make; you can't go wrong with a Porterhouse". You even recommend your favorite bottle of red wine to go with it.

Big Frankie's friend is now very happy and says "that sounds great Steve; I'll take the steak and bring us a couple bottles of that wine as well, thanks man". Score, you walk away thinking you did a great job and all is well. You can count the money now…but Big Frankie is not happy.

Remember, Big Frankie wants to be the star of the show not you. You just agreed with Frankie's buddy that he apparently can't choose a good dish. Then you one-upped him by going with a high ticket item like the Porterhouse and wine too. Big Frankie is not too happy 'cause you just showed him up. That steak better be great.

So now the food runner brings the meals out to Big Frankie's table. Since you are proud of your job you've done so far you walk with the runner, take the plates from him and serve the meals yourself. The runner is not too happy with you now because you just showed him up as well. Wow, tonight you're not making too many friends.

Knives and forks start on the food and you wait until the two bites are eaten before you leave. You've got the warm fuzzies now because you made their night. Yeah, who's the man? ME!

A little while later Big Frankie calls you over to complain about the Porterhouse. "Hey bud, you recommended that steak and my friend don't like it", he says. "Oh I'm very sorry what's wrong with the steak" you ask Frankie's friend. "He just don't like it, that's all" Frankie bellows, not even giving his friend a chance to speak. "Is it not cooked enough, I can get that refired for you if you want or is there anything else I can get for you" you say. "No, no, that's ok" his friend finally speaks up. "I'll just finish the mashed potatoes and bread" he says.

So you walk away from the table thinking that can't be right. Everybody loves the Porterhouse, why didn't this guy like it? Well maybe Big Frankie had something to do with it. You showed him up remember? But regardless, the guest didn't like the steak, and he proved it since half was left on his plate.

So now you just printed the check and sheepishly drop it on the table. "I'm not paying for that steak" Frankie says. "You recommended it and it wasn't good, I wanted to go with the veal chop" Frankie finishes.

Now you just lost. Not only have you potentially lost Big Frankie as a customer but you just lost the sale of the Porterhouse. There's no way you can keep that on the check. The guest only ordered the steak because you highly recommended it and said it melts in your mouth. Well not tonight, not for this guest.

Ok, here's the rule:

NEVER make a personal recommendation based on YOUR taste.

If YOU suggest a specific item and the guest doesn't like it, you may be obligated to remove the charge from the guest check. The reason is that the guest only ordered it because YOU recommended it.

Better option is to say:

- "Well, the Porterhouse steak IS one of our most popular items" or

- "Most of our customers have said great things about our Porterhouse, why don't you try it and judge for yourself?"

Regardless of what method you use, don't put yourself in a position where you may lose money. It's bad enough that you'll probably get stiffed on this table tonight but you just ruined the guest's dinner as well.

Remember, I'm here to show you how to earn bigger tips, not to lose them. Be smart and remember the guest is the star of the show not you. Inform them how the meals are prepared and what the sides are.

Let your manager, chef or sommelier recommend the specific food or wine to the guests. Then at least you the waiter don't get the blame in case they don't like it. Unless the guest is a jerk, you will still get a good tip. If not chalk it up to experience.

...but is there anything else you can get for them?

Is There Anything Else I May Get For You?

This is a quick one. You just dropped off the food to your guest, what do you do now? Do you just turn around and walk away? I hope not.

But let's back up a minute. When you presented the food to your guest, did you place the protein in the 6 o'clock position? You would be surprised how many servers are never taught this basic thing. Ever try to cut your food by reaching over your broccoli and red potatoes? It's not very graceful. Don't force the guest to rotate their plate either. Protein always goes at the 6'oclock position directly in front of the guest.

Did you inform the guest that the plate was hot, if that was the case? I'd be pretty pissed off too if my plate was hot and the server didn't tell me. The guest doesn't know that the cook places the plate with the sides under the broiler to keep warm while the protein is being finished. This makes for a hot plate. Make sure you tell the guest.

So you did all these thing right and the guest has their food.

> **NEVER walk away from the table without asking the guest if there is anything else you can get for them.**

Maybe they forgot to ask you for sour cream for their baked potato. And they realize it now. Maybe they forgot to mention that they didn't want onions on their Philly cheese steak, but they do now. Maybe they have almost finished their beverage, why don't you offer to refill it now.

You must never leave the table without making sure there is nothing else you can offer your guest. Offer a beverage refill. Offer them more bread and butter. Do they need another napkin, etc.

This is how you let your guests know that you are there to serve them, to take care of their needs. They let you know they appreciate it by leaving you a big tip.

...by the way, did the kids eat first?

Get That Kid His Mac & Cheese First

For those of you that have ever had to deal with a young child complaining about being hungry in a restaurant because their kids meal is not coming out fast enough, there is one sure fire way to fix it...

Get their meals first.

Great servers will automatically know to have the kitchen send out the kid's macaroni & cheese or chicken fingers with the first course salad for the adults without even having to ask. But ask you MUST.

"Ma'am, sir, do you want me to have the kids meal served right away, with your salad or would you like it to come with the other entrees?"

Depending on the age of the kids, most parents who bring their young children to a restaurant are just happy that they were able to get the kids out of the house and dressed in something nicer than their sweatpants or pj's. Then they are fighting with them to find something on the menu the kids will actually eat, or at least tolerate. They will not be focused on the timing of the meal.

So if you as a waiter just assume that you will have the kid's meal brought out with the other entrees you are not doing a service to the guest. Mom will spend most of her first course trying to explain to the little darling that his food "will be right out".

Sometimes the parent may want the child's meal to wait for whatever reason but usually they won't. This is why you must ask. Usually the parent will appreciate the fact that you understood the situation enough to think of this small item. But this is large on customer service.

Find out what the kid wants; ask if the parent wants their child's meal to be served as quickly as possible and ahead of theirs. Then get to your POS terminal and get the order in.

One last thing, **make sure you find a way to bring up your good deed to Mom or Dad**. When you are checking back with them in two minutes, say something like; "I'm glad we were able to get your son's mac & cheese out right away. We wouldn't want him to wait".

Since Mom now was able to enjoy her meal because her little one didn't have a hunger fit, she will help you enjoy YOUR day by counting her big tip.

...by now you're probably saying "I'm a waiter, not a salesman".

I'm a Waiter Not a Salesman!

Assume the sale. This is one of those phrases that is drilled into the head of any good salesperson. "They will love our product, I know they will. Just keep listing all the benefits of our product and they will have to buy it. So just assume that you will make the sale and ask them for their order", says the hungry sales manager boss.

Well I don't want you to be a hungry sales guy, at least not at this point. But I do want you to assume the sale. Here's what I mean.

Those well spoken of "two minutes or two bites" has quickly passed as you make your way to table #22. As you reach there you quickly scan the plates to see if the four guests are enjoying their meal. You say something like this:

- "Is everything ok"?

- "I hope you are enjoying the salmon"

No, no man that's all wrong. It's the worst way to check on a guest. Don't you know that everything is ok, were you paying attention? Why would you "hope" they like their salmon? This leaves doubt in the mind of the customer.

If you really were paying attention you would have checked on the dish before it left the kitchen. You would have made sure all the items on the plate are fresh and prepared the way the guest ordered.

When you are checking back with the guest, this is what I expect from you…

> **ALWAYS assume that their meal was exceptional and that they are happy with it.**

You, as a server, should be confident that the meal you presented to your guest is of the highest quality and that they will enjoy it

Use terms like:

- "I'm glad to see that you are enjoying your meal, is there anything else I may get for you?"

- "You made a great choice with that sea bass. I'm glad to see you liked it as well".

- "I can tell by the smile on your face you are enjoying the steak. Don't forget to save some room for one of our great desserts".

Can you think of any other statements that may be appropriate?

~~~~~~~~~~~~~~~~~~~~~~~~~~~~

Ok, I've been in this business too long to leave this chapter at this point. Many of you are probably saying "Sure it easy for you to say just be confident the meal is of the highest quality, blah blah blah, but you don't have to work with MY kitchen. They suck! "

"The cooks are always getting the orders wrong, we are always running out of items and the managers don't to a damn thing about it".

Well it sounds like your property is a loser. If this is the case you probably aren't making big tips anyway, so why are you still working there? You are better than that. What good is me helping you with your serving skills if your restaurant isn't there to back it up? You can't win, no way.

It's time to move on. Move on to another restaurant, bar or hotel that appreciates your skills, your service and your mindset.

> **You want to be the weakest server in the company. If that's the case then you know that you are surrounded with the best in the business and you can only get better.**

They will push you each day. You will learn additional skills from your co-workers every time you walk through that door. Skills that will also help you to be your best. Those losers from your old job will still be working for peanuts and you will move on to bigger and better things.

> **You will work with other professionals like yourself and will be proud of your job, your career and most of all proud of yourself as a person.**

You can't make the big tips working in a dump no matter how hard you try, no matter how many of my recommendations you follow.

Put yourself on a path to be successful and do it!

...even if it's your birthday!

Happy Birthday to You

I remember when I was around 18 or so, my friends and I used to go to the local hot-spot diner at all hours of the night for a cheese burger, fries with melted cheese and a soda. Comfort food and a few friends, what memories!

I also remember going to a few of those theme restaurants where they would get the whole wait staff to form a conga line of sorts and clap their hands in rhythm and sing happy birthday to some poor sole. You would hear this roar from the other side of the restaurant and just know that some kid was about to be humiliated. That wasn't their intention but it certainly was the result of this "good will".

In an effort I guess to make their customer's dining experience more friendly or to make them a part of the show these food eateries thought this nonsense was a good idea. But all it did was make their guests uncomfortable.

So as devious teenagers, my friends and I would take our revenge on society by mentioning to the hostess that today was the birthday of "our friend and we were sitting over at so and so table". She in turn would tell this to the server of that table and after a few minutes out would come all the pimply-faced waiters marching in a row and clapping like a bunch of circus seals. Singing happy birthday to you was the punishment these folks doled-out. The last person in the line would hold the free piece of birthday dessert and place it in front of the unsuspecting patron.

We would laugh our butts off at our escapades. I know that was not some major crime but it sure was fun. We reveled in the awkward 30 seconds or so we had just bestowed upon the unlucky chap. I think those waiters enjoyed their misery as well as we did.

So where am I going with this? Do I expect you to be a circus seal and sing happy birthday to them too? Of course not. But I do want you to acknowledge it.

If you have the unfortunate "pleasure" to work in one of the happy birthday torture chamber restaurants, or any time you find out that it's the birthday of one of your guests; this is what I want you to do:

Go up to the guest and wish them a happy birthday as well. Don't make a big deal of it just a sincere happy birthday will do.

~~~~~~~~~~~~~~~~~~~~~~~~~~

This rule goes for any other special event: anniversary, winning an award, etc. Just acknowledge the special day for them. I bet you have served countless guests over the years that have opened a gift at your table.

Did you bother to find out what the gift was for or if this was a special day for them? If not you missed a great opportunity to connect with your guest.

~~~~~~~~~~~~~~~~~~~~~~~~~~

When their meal is over and you present the check, make a point to wish them happy birthday again as you say goodbye. If it's a couple having a special anniversary dinner, wish them many more anniversaries. Be sincere, share their happiness.

> **Anytime you find out that it is a birthday, anniversary, etc. of a guest, ask the kitchen for a special desert and present it to the guest. Get your manager to do something different for them, even if it's just a free glass of wine to celebrate.**

They will always appreciate the special attention you gave them.

…and don't ruin it by talking about "your stuff".

I Have My Own Stuff to Talk About

When has it become acceptable to start or enter into a non work related conversation with a fellow server when you are "on the floor"?

You probably are saying "Ok here he goes, he's finally going to rip into us for something stupid". No, not at all.

How do you expect to realize if your guests are in need of something or if their food is waiting under the kitchen heat lamp when you're talking about your date last night or your favorite football team? The object of this book is to give you the tools and tactics needed to earn bigger tips. You won't get them if you are not paying attention to your guest!

"Yeah, but I just left my table, they were fine. I refilled their water and bread basket and asked if they needed anything else. What more do you want from me?" you may say.

> **I want you to be laser-focused on your job and your guests.**

Do you think that when some star baseball player is in the batting cage he is BS'ing about the vacation he just returned from? Do you think that when that lead guitarist from the big rock band is on stage he would lean over to his band mate to tell him about the new car he just bought? Do you think that actress on stage at the award show will pull out her cell phone and show us photos of her new puppy? I don't think so.

How do you think they got to where they are? By taking their job as serious as a heart attack.

By focusing on what they need to get better at and devoting all their efforts to make it happen. By paying attention to the task at hand.

YOUR task at hand is the guests at your table.

Remember, the customer doesn't care about your needs or your problems. They only care about their needs. Who can blame them? When you are waiting in that long line at the supermarket the day before a big holiday, do you care that the cashier has been standing there for the past 3 hours scanning items and filling bag after bag of groceries?

Heck no, you just want to get out of there. "What's taking her so long" you are saying to yourself. "I've got things to do and don't feel like spending all day here."

Well that's what your guests are saying to themselves as well when they are looking around the restaurant for you. "I want to place my order, where's the waiter?" "Can't I get a refill on my coffee, where's the waiter?" "Come on man; bring back my credit card I want to go home".

This is what's happening in the mind of your guest when you are not around and they need you. Don't get into side conversations with your server buddies, your guests don't care about that. Don't complain to your bartender friend about your problems, your guests don't care about that either.

A few other things your guests don't care about...

- Your alarm didn't go off so you overslept and were late for work. So now your boss gave you the worst closing assignments.

- You got stuck at your "other job" so you rushed over here and didn't have time to shave in between jobs. You look like hell. The guests should not have to be served by some scruffy-looking dude.

- You just had a fight with your boyfriend and are now mad at the world and really don't want to smile or use the "Magical Table Greeting."

- Your car got repossessed and you need to wait for a friend to take you home. She just called you to say she will be really late and that's going to mess up the rest of your day.

- Your mind is somewhere else because you have a lot of homework to do after your shift and finals are next week.

> **You may have your own stuff to talk about but not during working hours. If you want the big tips, talk with your guests.**

Be professional. Describe a few of the dishes in detail to them. Show them you know the menu like the back of your hand. They may want to try something different. Tell them about the history of the restaurant. Let them know about any upcoming special promotions planned.

Be "a person" to your guests, not just "the waiter". The customer will like a waiter but feel a connection to "a person". Treat them well and they will treat YOU well.

...and make sure you know thy substitutions.

Know Thy Substitutions

No matter how much planning went into developing and designing the menu by your chef or owner, there will always be some customers that don't want the asparagus or fingerling potatoes that comes with their entrée. Inevitably some customer will ask you "Can I get broccoli or mashed potatoes instead"? That's only normal and should be expected.

So do you know what your options are? Do you know what other side dishes are always available that may not be on the menu? Do you know if any special vegetables were delivered earlier today that may be available tonight? If not, there goes another opportunity to WOW your guest.

"Well we have broccoli, corn, or patty-pan squash if you like" is the usual comeback. Not as the other available sides but the manner in which the server will respond to the guest. I have a better way of answering this question from the guest.

> **"Let me go and speak with our chef. I did see some special vegetables (or potatoes) were delivered earlier today that are not usually on our menu. Maybe I can get him to prepare them for you". Let me see what magic I can do?**

Now, if you were the customer and your waiter just said this to you, how would you feel? You would feel great. You would feel special. You have a great waiter. One that is going out of his way to talk with the chef and get him to part with his "special veggies" just for you!

Can't you just smell the big tip!

Now whether there are any special veggies or not, you better come back to the table with good news. Good news and a big smile - because you know you just clinched the deal for the guest.

> "Well we're in luck" you say. "I was able to convince my chef to take some of his prized zucchini that he was saving for a special dish tomorrow. He will slice it thin and cook it with some white wine and butter. It should taste great."
>
> "Or he has some baby carrots and string beans, we can sauté them with garlic and maybe add some teriyaki sauce for a little Asian flavor if you like".

There's the WOW factor! Now you did it! It will now be very hard for your guest to turn down one of your special substitutions. You went out of your way to talk your chef into doing something special for you…how can he say no?

And even if your guest is not interested in one of your new sides, he will remember your efforts later.

The final kicker is this:

When you present the check make a subtle reminder of what you did for him.

> "Here is your check and thank you for your business. I'm very happy we were able to get you those special vegetables. When you come back next time I'll see what else the chef has for you".

Now THAT's magic, almost as good as my table greeting! You definitely won this customer over and they will leave your restaurant remembering a good meal, a flexible chef and a GREAT waiter.

Your good deed will not be forgotten. Money Money Money!

Now you must do your homework in order for this to work as described. You can't just barge into your kitchen and expect your chef to go out of his way during the middle of service to make some special side dish for you. It just won't happen. So let me tell you how this came about.

~~~~~~~~~~~~~~~~~~~~~~~~~~~

Years ago I had a very ambitious waiter working for me, he was great. Never satisfied with the usual way of doing things, always looking for another option.

He would go into the kitchen each night and talk with the cooks to see what else they had. If he got nowhere with them he would go into the chef's office and speak directly with him.

"Hey chef, in case any of our customers ask me tonight, are there any other options I can give them for the veggies or pasta we have?" "A few times this week I got special requests for things like orecchiette or angel-hair pasta and then even zucchini last night" he says. "I know we don't usually have these items but are there any other things you may have that I can offer our guests if they ask?

It's hard to turn down a request like this from a good server especially if it's asked in a way that has the best intentions for our customers. Our chef found some other items to offer that night. Then it got interesting.

Before long, we started to notice a few more, then a lot more, options to offer as side dishes. Prior to our pre-shift meeting, my waiter was getting together every few days with the chef and talked him into trying some new items each week. He even went so far as to offer daily specials of veggies and 3 different pasta dishes as entrees. They were some of our best sellers.

I promoted that waiter to lead server and then eventually junior manager. I heard he was later moved up to full manager a short time after I left. Good for him, he deserved it. He's probably the head of some Fortune 500 company now. I may need to go work for him soon.

~~~~~~~~~~~~~~~~~~~~~~~~~~~

So if you want to try this you need to do your homework. Find out each day what your potential substitutions are. Find out if the cooks will actually make it for you. If not speak with the chef.

Hopefully you will have one that is open-minded like the one I had and made it easy for us. And easy for the waiters to make big tips.

...even if you don't know where you left that thing.

Where Did I Leave That Thing?

Have you ever asked one of your coworkers where do we keep the horseradish? Where's the to-go boxes? I can't find any more check presenters, have you seen one around here?

While you are trying to get answers to questions like these, your guests are patiently waiting. How long do you think is appropriate to keep them waiting? Not a moment longer than necessary.

But wait they will if you don't know where your equipment is, if you don't know where you keep the horseradish. Remember, when a guest is waiting for ketchup to put on her fries or another napkin to wipe their mouth, 15 seconds seems like an eternity. They want what they want when they want it!

So much time is spent on teaching new waiters the daily specials, or how to use the Micros terminal to enter the food orders, or to spout the company B.S. that everything else is forgotten.

What good is all of this if the waiters don't know where to go to get certain additional food items or paper products to service their customer?

> **You need to be the complete package, the 'go to' waiter. The one that knows all the tricks and all the secret hiding places.**

If not what will you do? Just wander around the kitchen or the rear storeroom hunting through boxes for more kid sippy cups? If no one restocked the cups you are the one that suffers because you can't find one for the little girl at your table. And she suffers as well.

Familiarize yourself with the various storage areas for all food and non-food items.

You never know when you may be asked for something out of the ordinary by a guest. When it happens you will be better prepared to retrieve it and give to your guest quickly.

Make sure all equipment is put back in its correct storage area after each use.

Remember: everything has its place. All too frequently equipment never gets put back correctly where it belongs. Either because the person doesn't know where it belongs or they are too lazy.

Even if you go to the right storage area to pick up the bar tray or wooden pepper mill, you will come up empty if the last user didn't put it back.

The manager needs to train the employees where EVERYTHING goes and give a swift kick to the backside of the lazy ones.

Get friendly with the person responsible for purchasing all the products.

Reach out to the purchaser and get in good with him. He will know where things are. Ask him for a tour of the dry goods room. Explain your reasons: because you want to make sure you know where stuff is in case you get a last minute request for something that is not already in rotation. He should offer to help you.

Learn who the various supervisors are within other departments and what their areas of responsibility are.

Example:

You are a hotel room service waiter that just got an order for coffee and juice for a group of 11 people. You don't have a large enough coffee pot or juice pitcher to take care of this and you can't use all the smaller pots. That will clean you out and you won't have enough equipment for the other rooms.

What do you do? The customer is waiting...

Find the banquet manager, or banquet captain, and explain your situation. Ask him if you can borrow one of his larger coffee pots or juice pitchers for your order. Unless they are super busy he will not say no. Tell him how much you appreciate it and that you will return the pots as soon as possible. And MAKE SURE you do.

When you return them ask the manager if it would be ok to borrow them again if you get another large order.

Now you have a contact in the Banquet Department to help you in the future. The better action would have been to make this contact much earlier. A great room service waiter would have reached out to the banquet staff when he first started so he could be prepared when the larger orders come...and come they will.

This all leads to satisfying the needs to the customer quickly. All this behind the scenes effort will never be known by your guest. But they will know if you haven't taken the efforts ahead of time.

Be prepared for your guests and their unexpected requests.

...by the way where's my busboy?

My Busboy, My Partner

How do you treat your busser? Do you treat him/her as a partner? Do you treat him with respect and train him how to do the job better?

Now you're probably saying "You expect ME to train the busboy"? "That's not my job the managers need to do that". So what if your managers didn't train him well, the manager still gets paid, you don't!

You're tips will suffer because your success as a waiter is heavily dependent upon the work the busboy does.

Do you think you will receive a big tip if the guest is always out of water or has dirty plates in front of them? I doubt it. But if your restaurant is designed where the bussers pour the water, get the bread and clear plates, you're screwed. If the busser is not doing it...are you?

You should get your busboy involved in what you do. Teach him a modified version of the magical table greeting. When he goes to the table he should introduce himself as well and MUST have a big smile.

If it's your guest's birthday, tell your busboy. Let him share that special day with your guest as well. You can't afford him being some silent partner or a robot that goes from table to table just pouring water and taking dirty plates. That is not service. That is not how you get a big tip.

Everyone that meets your guest needs to do their part in order for you to hit the ball out of the park.

Even if your restaurant doesn't have a good training program, YOU must be the trainer. YOU must be the one to teach your busser what he or she needs to know in order to take care of the guest.

They are customers of the restaurant but they are YOUR guests!

If your restaurant "auctions the food" (asking the guests "Who gets the hamburger, who ordered the fish"), you must not allow this to happen to you guests. Teach the busser seat assignments. Teach the food runner seat assignments, especially the food runner.

Show him the correct side of the guest to clear dirty plates. Show him how to use spoons instead of tongs when he is "Frenching" the bread. Show him how to open a bottle of wine and maybe even the correct way to pour it tableside. What! Have my busboy pour the wine for me, are you CRAZY!

Well maybe on that busy Saturday night when you are "in the weeds" you busser can come to your rescue. But it will never happen if you don't train him.

So let's assume you have done as I asked and you have trained your busser to be the best in the restaurant. Now use this to your advantage and take this a step further.

~~~~~~~~~~~~~~~~~~~~~~~~

Talk him up to your table. How many times has this happened to you?

You are taking the guest's orders when your busser comes to the table to fill the guest's water glasses? What do you do? Do you ignore him and continue to take the orders? I hope not.

You should stop what you are doing and introduce your busser to your guests. Yes you heard right! Try this...

> Oh, this is Jose, he is the best busser on our restaurant
> and he's working with me today. He's my partner and we
> both are here to take care of you. So if there is anything you
> need and you can't find me for any reason, please reach out
> to Jose and he will take care of it.

Now, two things just happened…

Your guests know that they have two people servicing them today. That will make them feel comfortable, maybe even special. And you have also lifted the esteem of your busser.

How many waiters have EVER introduced the busboy to their table? I will safely say zero!

You have just gained a busboy for life. He will go out of his way to watch your table, to make sure your guests (and his) are satisfied. He will want to work with only one waiter from this point on, YOU!

So when you get your big tip, you MUST NOT be cheap with your tip-outs. Make sure your best busser is well compensated. You will make up for this each day Jose is working with you.

He will not let you down, nor will your guests.

…what are they looking for, a book store?

Where's The Nearest Bookstore?

Do you know the other businesses around your restaurant or hotel? Are you one of those that just drive straight from your home to work without noticing what's around you? If so then snap out of it!

> **You need to be a fountain of knowledge... and I don't mean about the menu.**

If your guest at table 14 was interested in buying a gift for a friend of theirs and asked you if you knew where the nearest bookstore or men's clothing store was could you steer them in the right direction? Or would you say "I'm not from around here, sorry". You should be ashamed of yourself.

Would you give that same lame excuse to one of your friends? Or to your grandma? Heck no! You would go out of your way to find the answer. You would ask someone else, get out the telephone book or of course get on the internet, plug in your zip code and search through countless results to pick the best store nearest you.

Would you do this for the lady at table 14? Now I realize it's not practical to expect you to go searching the web during your shift to help your guest, but what if you did? What if you didn't know where the nearest book store was but you DID want to help your guest?

Maybe you could tell your manager about this and get permission to do just that, search the web. After all, you are doing your best to satisfy the needs of your customer right?

Use your phone or the nearest office computer but do it fast! Plug in the info, get the answer and rush back to your table and say...

> **"I'm sorry I didn't have the answer for you right away but I asked my manager if I could use his computer to search for the nearest book store and he said yes".**
>
> **"There is a big store only a mile and a half away from here and they are open until 9pm. I take a different route when I come to work so I don't pass it but now we BOTH know where the book store is. Hopefully you can find the book you are interested in".**

Can you imagine the surprise you just gave to your guest? Would they have ever dreamed that you would have followed up on this after you said "you were not from around here"? Never in a million years.

That's how you WOW a guest.

Now this scenario may not be possible in your establishment. Maybe you have a jerk boss that is not interested in WOWing the customers and won't let you get on the computer. But there is another way to get the answer for your guests though it's not as good as the computer.

Over the next several days or weeks, take a different route to work if possible. Notice the other businesses that are near your job. Think of the type of shopping your guests may be interested in and want to go to after they had a meal in your restaurant.

Would they look for a book store? You know where that one is now. Maybe they're running out of gas and need to fill up. Tell them where the closest station is. Maybe they decided to pass on dessert with you and just wanted to take a stroll to help digest their food. Why not tell them where the nearest park is. You know, the one with the small lake and pretty ducks. You've gone there yourself.

52

> **Anytime your guest asks you a question about something you should be able to give them an accurate answer.**

It may not be the exact answer they were looking for but sometimes it is the effort you gave to try to help your guest that matters. They would welcome an answer, almost any answer, over a blank stare and an I don't know comment.

Now if you were this customer, would you expect to reward this nice waiter with a big fat tip for his efforts?

...do they even need to ask for it?

Do They Really Need To Ask For It?

I'm thirsty, where's that damn waiter! Now you're looking around the restaurant, can't find him. Your food is good but you need something to wash it down with. You finished your beer and want another. Where's that waiter? Honey, do you see him anywhere? This sucks man. There goes his tip! What? I gotta tip this guy for this and he's not around anywhere? No way! Hey, is that Jose the busboy? I'll ask HIM for another beer.

Now as you pass by this table, the thirsty guest flags you down to let you know that he needed another beer and couldn't find you. But he did find super busboy Jose and asked him for it. "Oh great, I'm glad Jose was able to get that for you" you say as you walk away. Now you are thinking "Boy that Jose is great. I trained him well and he got that guest the beer, well done". You think you did a good job and set yourself up for success because now you have a "partner" to help you with your tables.

You add the beer to the guest check and later present it to your table. The guest pays the bill and gives you a crappy tip. What happened?

"He wanted another beer, so I wasn't around but Jose got it for him. What's the big deal, why did he stiff me"? "We did everything correct, right?" WRONG?

> **Yes, your busser is your partner but he or she is not the one responsible for getting the guest his beverage refill, YOU ARE!**

As a busser, depending on the establishment, Jose is responsible for refilling water glasses and getting more bread and butter, not for serving alcoholic drinks. Many places will fire a busser for even touching a beer.

You, the waiter, must continually monitor your table to make sure they are happy with their food AND to make sure they have a full beverage.

> **Do you continually refill your guest's water glass? "Oh that's the busser's job". Well there goes your tip. Do you continually replenish the bread or crumb the table? "Oh that's the busser's job. Again, there goes your tip.**

I can't tell you how many times I've heard a waiter say things like this to their busser:

"Table 24 needs more water"

"Get more butter for table 15 please"

"I need you to bring 6 wine glasses to number 33 quick?

This drives me nuts!

What are you doing? Don't tell me you are so busy just taking orders that you can't refill a water glass. Oh, you have an 8 table section and you're in the weeds. You're running around like a nut just getting the orders in, you can't get their water? This happens every day.

Is this how you want to work, like an animal? Are you a professional? Of course you are; we've already gone over that. You provide great customer service (especially after reading this book!) and should be working in a place that will allow you to act as one.

Do you have an 8 table section because you need to cover for a server that called out sick? That's understandable. But many times servers will con their inexperienced managers into thinking they can handle a bigger section. Just because they think this will make them more money. YOU ARE WRONG!

Give me a 3 or 4 table section any day and I will prove I will make more in tips than another waiter that has 8.

Note: Of course this is not possible when working in a low-end restaurant with $14.95 entrees.

A smaller section allows you to interact with your guest, if that is appropriate. It allows you more time to observe their meal, to anticipate their needs, to sell them a bottle of wine.

Ah, to sell a bottle of wine. This is the best and easiest way to increase your tip. We will get into that later in this book.

We're getting off track; let's get back to your table...

The guest will appreciate the busser coming by to constantly refill their water glass or take their dirty plates. But they are not tipping the busser. Who should be the one that gets the credit for taking care of the guest, you or the busser? You or the food runner?

If the food is good the chef gets the credit but YOU get the tip. Your job is the best in the world. Someone else cooks the food, another person delivers the food, another guy clears the dirty dishes and YOU get the tip. What a country we have!

Getting a big tip is not automatic just because of one or two good things that happen at the table. It's a complete package of actions taken by all the people that come into contact with the customer from the moment they enter the door. And many times even BEFORE they enter the door. They will have certain expectations of your business even as they make the reservation over the phone.

Sometimes one little less-than-perfect thing is enough to give a customer a reason to give you a 15% tip instead of 20% tip or more. I'll take that extra 5% every time. But you need to work for it. 15% is not enough.

So you must do a few simple things for each and every table you have to make sure your guests don't need to round-up a search party just to get a beer.

> **Your guest should NEVER need to ask for a beverage refill.**

If your guest must seek you out for a water, soda, or wine refill then you are not doing your job. You are not being attentive enough. Now speaking of wine...

> **Sell that second bottle of wine.**

Your 4-top ordered a bottle of wine, great. You poured four full glasses of wine and the bottle is finished. YOU LOST AGAIN!

You NEVER finish the bottle of wine for 4 guests!

You always leave enough in the bottle so when you go to refill the glasses..."Oh I'm sorry, would you like me to get you another bottle of wine"? How can they say no? You already poured part of the potential 5th glass to one of the guests. It's a sure thing and more money for you. But not if you finish the bottle on the first round.

> **You must ALWAYS offer a second cup of coffee or tea.**

Coffee is the start and finish of the dessert service. Once you take their dessert order, the first thing that comes to the table is the coffee. Then the dessert is offered.

Then you must check back on your guests (2 minutes or 2 bites, remember?).

When it looks like they are almost finished with their coffee, you DO NOT go up to the table empty handed and ask them if they want more coffee. You must assume they want it. Greet your table with the coffee pot in hand and offer more coffee. If they don't want any more that's fine. But the dessert service is not complete unless a second cup is offered.

By the way...

> **Did you offer a cappuccino or espresso instead? Don't these cost more than regular coffee? UPSELL man! Get that check average up. Bigger check, bigger tip!**

Ok, ok, let's continue.

Did you give them enough sugar, milk or cream for the second round of coffee? I bet not. Especially if your place uses those dopey little single-serve creamer cups with the paper pull-top. I hate these things. Nothing is cheesier than these cups. That's what I expect from a school cafeteria not a fine dining establishment.

But maybe you don't work in a fine dining establishment. Maybe this is how you do it, so ok, what can I do?

Just make sure that if your guests are getting a second round of coffee you provide them with additional sugar, milk or creamer. That's it.

And DON'T make them ask for it!

...now get outta my way!

Now Get Outta My Way!

This chapter is a little more fitting for my banquet waiter friends. Ah, the banquet waiters. I could write a book just about them, and I probably will sometime.

A banquet waiter is the hardest working waiter in the business. Yeah, I bet that pissed-off you a la carte gals. If so I'm sorry.

In case you aren't aware, in the banquet world there are no bussers, no runners and no hostesses. They do it all. So it's understandable if they run around like a chicken at times. This is when it gets hairy.

To you a la carte servers, see if these scenarios apply to you as well.

~~~~~~~~~~~~~~~~~~~~~~~~~~~~

Ever been so busy at work that you don't seem to look around? You are focused on your task at hand and are making good time but still are trying to rush to get something done. Does this sound familiar?

Scenario #1

You are running food for the buffet today. You realize that the chaffer of chicken is almost finished so you rush into the kitchen for more. You pull the back-up pan from the hot box, rip off the plastic wrap and bolt through the kitchen door and into the room. **BAM**, you run into a guest that is walking past the doors and spill the gravy all over him/her.

Scenario #2

You are clearing glasses from the cocktail area and make a point to arrange them securely on the cocktail tray. You're an experienced waiter and know how to carry a tray (good for you). Then as you lift the tray off the table and pivot around to leave, you bump into a guest that has inadvertently walked into your intended path to the kitchen. Down went all the glasses. You watch as they shatter on the floor.

Scenario #3

You have a "football tray" full of food for your table and you set it down on your tray stand. You didn't think it would be a big deal so you dropped it in the spot that was most convenient for you, right in the middle of an aisle. Oh no...

As you present the first plate to your table, out of the corner of your eye you see some linebacker-sized dude trying to squeeze between your tray stand and the table next to it. This is not good.

You reach for the tray in the hopes of steadying it but no, you're too slow. The guy belly bumps the tray and down it goes. Along with the rest of your table's food. He does apologize but who cares?

Three things I hope never happen to you. But happen it does.

The most important thing to remember when in the middle of service is to PAY ATTENTION to your surroundings and DON'T RUSH.

LOOK to see what obstacles are near.

OPEN all doors slowly and under control.

ALWAYS be aware of who may be next to you.

NEVER be so rushed that you cut-off a guest or rush in front of them.

The guest ALWAYS has the right-of-way through any door, corridor or walkway. You may want to get to your table quickly but not at the expense of dropping something, banging into a guest or worst of all spilling their food on the floor or them.

I remember being an 18 year old banquet waiter at a catering hall in Brooklyn New York. Yes, I'm a Brooklyn boy!

Anyway, we used to get the wedding cake cut in our kitchen, plate it on small plates then arrange them in sets of 10 on our trays. We would then place the trays on a rolling cart and wheel it into the ballroom. Seems kind of silly now but that was the how we did it.

There was a time when I was trying to squeeze my cart between two tables and didn't fit. I will always remember the white cake icing being smeared all over the collar of 2 fur coats that were draped on the back of chairs. Yes fur coats! Why the heck didn't these ladies put them in the coat check?

I was mortified and didn't know what to do. I panicked and did what any good 18 year old from Brooklyn would do. I got the hell outta there!

I served that table as fast as I could and spent the rest of the night in the kitchen. I don't think I went near that table until the band played their last song.

Well, that's my story. What's yours?

You don't want to sacrifice your tip because you dropped a guest's meal on the floor and made them wait for a re-fire. You don't want to lose your tip because you did ANYTHING to upset a guest.

Especially by crashing into them.

...and don't crash into their camera.

Take My Picture, Please?

How can any waiter refuse a request like this. "Hey waiter, can you please take a picture of us, it's our anniversary"? Of course you say yes and take the camera in your steady hands. You do your best to not cut their heads off in the photo. You probably even took a good shot, well done.

But what if your guest didn't ask you to take their picture? Would you even ask them? If you happen to notice a camera lying on the table or placed next to your guest why not bring it up? Ask your guests if they would like their picture taken.

"I noticed you have a camera with you", you say. I would be happy to take a nice photo of you if you like". What a nice thing to offer to a guest.

"Oh, no that's ok" your guest says. Or "Why yes, could you do that for us"? That would be great!

So you carefully take their camera and snap off a shot or two. You may even recommend a nicer backdrop in another area of the restaurant if possible. Just get that shot.

They thank you for taking their photo and continue with their meal. You say "You're welcome" and walk away. So now are you finished with this right? No, no, no.

> **You must bring this up again later when you drop the check!**

> **You see, this is a sneaky little trick that almost always works. Anytime you do something special for a guest, and I mean special, remember to mention it again to the guest.**

"I'm glad I was able to get a nice photo earlier of you two on your anniversary, it's always nice to remember special days like this. Here's your check."

"I'm glad we were able to get the chef to part with his special veggies for your meal. It wasn't easy but it was worth the effort. "Here's your check".

"I'm glad I was able to find the nearest bookstore for you before. Be careful driving there. Here's your check".

Get the idea?

> **Just as you give the guest their check, reinforce a positive action you did earlier.**

This should make them want to be generous towards you. Even if it doesn't, it will still leave a memory in the minds of your guests. They will remember this as they walk out the door.

A memory of a great waiter, YOU.

...oh, did you sell them any wine?

Sell the Wine Every Time

If you are not selling wine at your tables you are missing out on one of the easiest ways to raise your check average and your tips. And I know why many waiters don't do this. They are afraid to!

"I don't know much about wine".

"I always have a problem opening the bottles".

"I'd just rather push the desserts".

If excuses like this come from you it's time to stop and stop now!

Selling wine is one of the easiest things to do and the best way to increase your tips. You don't need to be a sommelier and know every possible varietal and can tell the difference between the types of dirt the grapes were grown in. Who has time for that stuff? Not you.

But there are certain things you must learn about wine in order to sell it. But it's easy.

> **Just learn a little about two white and two red wines that are offered in your restaurant.**

That's it. No more no less.

Pick two good and average priced wines from your list. Wines that are readily available and judged as quality by most people. Learn about them. Buy one of those "Wine for Dummies" books. Invest in yourself for once in your life. It will pay off. I promise.

Is the wine sweet, or dry? Is it full bodied, fruity or have a hint of oak? What type of food to they pair well with? It's not that difficult.

Then for a little more knowledge, learn how to decant a wine. Learn the difference between a Bordeaux or Burgundy wine glass. Learn about the wine aroma wheel. You can go on forever, but don't bother. Just knowing enough about a few wines will cover most guests that enter your average restaurant. If your guest is looking for something different, more exotic than you know, enlist the help of your manager or even the bartender.

Selling wine is a profitable business. So good that at least one "Italian themed" restaurant presets all their tables with a wine glass, places tent cards about wine on the table and has the waiter greet you with a carafe of house wine in his hand. That's a little too much for my taste but they must be doing it for a reason. It makes money!

Think about how much your tips will increase if you sold just 1 bottle of $40 wine to each table. "Oh but I usually work the lunch shift, they will never order wine", you are saying. Well, did you try, then how do you know? How can you be so sure and so closed-minded?

Ever hear about the "2 martini lunch" taken by thousands of business people each day? Well why can't it be a "bottle of wine lunch"? Why can't you sell a bottle of wine to 3 ladies that have just completed a great day of clothes shopping and are looking for a nice late lunch to finish it off? Offer them a glass of wine, and if they are interested upsell that to a bottle.

Ok so we've taken care of the first excuse about not knowing enough about wine. Now let's move on to the next. You always have a problem with the corks when you open a bottle. Well that's one of the easiest to fix.

Come in a little earlier each day and offer to open all the wine bottles for your bartender. They won't mind and you will become an expert at this after only 1 week!

Now when you sell that nice bottle of wine you will have the confidence to open the bottle table-side without the fear of looking foolish. Present the wine correctly, offer a tasting to the guest that placed the order, then pour for the guests. But remember what I said in an earlier chapter...

NEVER finish a bottle of wine for 4 guests!

If a table orders a bottle of wine, maybe they will want another. When pouring you must always leave enough in the bottle to refill their glasses. But it's impossible to get another round of 4 out of one bottle. This is where your skill comes in.

Your guests should not have to refill their glass, that's your job. So when you come back around, take it upon yourself to lift the almost empty bottle and start filling their glasses. They will let you know if they don't want more. But if they do you will not get more than 1 additional glass full before you're empty. Now ask the host of the table or the person that ordered the wine if they will like to order an additional bottle. It's as easy as that.

The second excuse is done now. You are an expert wine bottle opener and learned a little tactic to get that second bottle sold. On with number 3. You would rather just push the desserts than sell wine.

Well that's great, upsell the desserts all day long. But I bet you won't be relying on the desserts to up your checks as much now because wine is your new friend. A friend that makes you more money.

Plus would you rather hope to sell 4 desserts that still cost less than 1 bottle of wine? So you don't push the wine because you are waiting to upsell them desserts. That's fine but what if their entrée is finished, they don't want dessert and ask you for their check? You can't go back and sell that bottle of wine now. You lost the opportunity. And the desserts are gone too.

Push the wine at the beginning of the meal and lay the foundation for a nice check. Then later when they order dessert and a cappuccino that's a bonus. If not at least you have already sold a bottle of wine.

You put your success in your hands. Not in the hands of the kitchen.

What if they did order desserts but by now the kitchen is getting busy and the desserts take a little too long to be made. The guest will wait and your tip will suffer. You went out of your way all evening long to do a great job, and you did. But now the last part of the meal is delayed because the kitchen is swamped with dessert orders.

I'll sell the wine any day.

...well it's time to say goodnight.

Goodnight My Guest

Y ou have just completed a great service at your table. You followed all the company's service standards and the food was presented well. You sold them 2 bottles of wine, crumbed the table between courses and even took their picture. Your guests had a wonderful time tonight and it was obvious from their smiles.

Did you say goodbye and thank them for coming? If not, WHY?

You have just spent an hour or more with these customers, YOUR guests, and didn't think it was appropriate or NECESSARY to wish them a good afternoon/goodnight and a safe trip home? Is this how you treat a guest at YOUR HOUSE?

I hope not! Your grandma would be ashamed of you.

Plus, saying goodnight will not help you to earn more tips if you say this AFTER your guest has paid their bill and are already walking towards the door. This must be said BEFORE you present the check.

You can't drop the check, collected the payment and then walk away from your guests and hide in the back of the back-of-house area waiting for them to leave.

Do NOT start your closing side-work so you can go home earlier.

Do NOT lose interest in this table and move your focus onto

another table and group. You have not finished the service with this table, these guests. You are not finished with them until they walk out the door. Never forget that.

You want the last thing your guests experience, their exit, to be as memorable as their entrance and greeting was.

As you go to your table, and while still holding the guest check in your hands, THIS is the time to send them off on a happy note.

This is the time to "clinch-the-deal! This is when you make your final pitch to your guests and butter them up with praise and appreciation.

It works, I promise.

Thank them for coming.

Say "It was a pleasure taking care of you today/tonight".

Offer to get their coats from the coat check room. Help put their coat on, assist them with their bags, open the door for them, etc.

Wish them a sincere good afternoon, goodnight, etc.

Ask them to return again with a comment like:

- "I hope you can join us again".

- "Hope to see you again soon".

- "When you come back, please ask for me. I will be happy to take care of you again".

Let your guests know that you were happy they came and that you had the opportunity to serve them. Be appreciative of the big tip you will soon receive.

THEN you drop the check!

> **I know you would do this if you had a dinner party at your house and it was time for your friends or family to leave. Right?**

You would wrap up some food in aluminum foil or "Tupperware" and put them in the nicest bags you have. Never those yellow plastic supermarket bags. Oh no.

You would make sure they didn't have too much to drink and were ok to drive. You would get their coats and hand them out one by one. You have a big warm hug ready as well.

You would get your shoes on and even walk them to their car carrying the doggie bags. You would place them gently in the trunk and help grandma into her seat and maybe even try to assist her with the seat belt...until she said 'That's ok honey I can do it". One final hug and kiss to all.

Then as the car drives away you are left standing at your door or in the driveway waving as they move out of sight. They know you appreciated them being there. You showed them in countless ways.

Can't you do this for your guests at work as well?

...a customer or a guest?

Why Do I Keep Referring To The Customer As Guest?

G ood question, why is that? What is the difference? Does it even matter?

Definition of Customer*

a) One that purchases a commodity or service

b) An individual usually having some specified distinctive trait

Example: A real tough customer

Definition of a Guest*

a) A person entertained in one's house

b) A person to whom hospitality is extended

c) A person who pays for the services of an establishment (as a hotel or restaurant)

You should clearly see the difference.

Our place of business should be treated as if it was our house, with all the same respect and diligence of our home.

*By permission. From Merriam-Webster's Collegiate® Dictionary, 11th Edition ©2013 by Merriam-Webster, Inc. (www.Merriam-Webster.com).

We extend hospitality to the people that enter our home. We would never let someone leave our home angry or upset because their needs or wishes were not fulfilled.

> These "customers" are paying for the services that are provided in our house. They deserve to be treated as WE would want to be treated when we go out, when we are "the guest".

Treat them in a way that will ensure their repeat business.

...do I REALLY care about my guest?

Do I Really Care About My Guest?

How do you really feel about your guests? How far will you go to serve them? When is "good enough" NOT good enough? Will you go the extra mile, even if it's not really that far after all?

So again I ask, do you REALLY care about your guests? Can you agree with these statements?

If I care I would NOT:

- Only brew regular coffee and tell the guest it's decaf
- Put my fingers inside the glasses or cups as I'm setting the table
- Put out a stained napkin
- Store wine bottles inside the ice bin
- Use the glass when I scoop ice from the bin instead of using a proper non-breakable scooper
- "Push the specials" when I know they are old and should be thrown in the garbage instead
- Touch my hair, blow my nose or adjust my clothes without next washing my hands
- Serve food to my guest when I know it's not presented well, and as per our standards, or is of inferior quality

If I did care I WOULD:

- Make sure their needs came before my needs

- Leave my problems at home

- Make sure my uniform, hair, etc were clean, neat and up to standards

- Not expect my busboy to be my slave and will fill your water glass myself

- Pour-off some soda when using the soda gun and then fill the glass. This way no old soda is poured in this glass

- Brush my teeth or take a breath mint PLUS wash my hands after smoking a cigarette

- Put some lemon in the hot water I use when polishing your silverware

- Look at the reservations already booked to be prepared for the next table or shift

- Never give you a dirty or less than full salt or pepper shaker

...it's a win win situation.

It's a Win Win Situation!

I hope you take the tips, tricks and recommendations from this book and use them today. And tomorrow, and the day after...

If you do, there is no way you can't earn bigger tips on your very next shift.

Don't write me letters saying "It's too hard to do, I can't say these things". Or "How am I supposed to remember all this"? That's nonsense. You're giving up before you even started.

Someone else may say to start slow and only use one or two of my suggestions. Then when you are more comfortable throw in another and so on. Well that IS better than nothing. You will get a bigger tip now and then. But why stop there? Is that all you want?

So study hard my friend. Learn fast. Don't procrastinate.

Hit the guest with 6 or 7 of these beauties right away. Do it today or tonight when you go to work. Don't chicken out. Make it happen!

Run these scenarios through your mind as you drive to work. Don't bother with the radio, that won't make you more money. Think of what you will say to the very first table you get tonight.

If you don't use my "Magical Table Greeting" on your first table you are doomed to fail.

You will have wasted your money on this book. Money you won't get back from your small tips.

But if you do follow my book and master these tactics, you will become the star performer of your restaurant. Every other waiter will be jealous of you because you make more than they do. Every busser will want to only work with you because you are their mentor. You have helped their self esteem. You have trained them better than your manager has. You have earned their respect. They will not let you down and will pay attention to your guests as much as you do.

You will be the customer service king. You now receive the most letters of praise from your guests. Repeat guests ask to be seated in your section. They may even ask you what days you work, so they can come back when you are in. That's a very nice complement.

And you're making money, more than you did before you bought this book. Not a bad deal, right?

~~~~~~~~~~~~~~~~~~~~~~~~~~~~~

Throughout these pages did I once talk about the skills usually taught to a waiter? Like how to hold the plates or a tray? Did I say you needed to memorize your menu and learn the 5 "mother sauces" so you can describe the food and its preparation just like the chef? Did I ask you to learn French so you can sound like a fancy schmancy waiter? No I didn't.

You don't need any of that stuff. That's what most people expect from a so called "great waiter". But that won't make you big tips.

> **Only by making your guests feel special, feel as if THEIR enjoyment is YOUR primary concern, will you make the big tips. All else is not important.**

Ok, so let's assume (there goes that word again) you follow my book to the "T" and become a service king. What or who else benefits from this? Your restaurant of course! With great customer service comes more business and more money for the company.

There is no way your manager would allow a waiter with your skills to not be noticed, to not be taken care of. At least with a good manager, and yes the good ones ARE hard to find these days.

If I was your manager I would do all I could to learn from you and put your skills to good use. I would ask you to take part in customer service training for your fellow employees based on your methods of dealing with the guest. Maybe you can even teach it. I would talk-you-up to the owner or the corporate big shots.

I want you to be promoted, promoted to lead server or captain. Maybe even manager if you are looking to switch to the "dark-side" as I always joke. Any business is foolish if a great employee like you is not taken care of and supported.

> **Before long there would be an army of waiters, bartenders, bussers & food runners working for them all with one thing in common. A MINDSET of SERVICE!**

~~~~~~~~~~~~~~~~~~~~~~~~~~~~~

This was MY motivation for writing this book. Yes I want all waiters to earn more tips, I really do. As I said earlier, a waiter that makes a good living is a happy waiter. And he or she does a better job.

But at the same time I want to raise the service level of all people in the hospitality industry. That's been my goal wherever I've worked. Whether you are a front desk agent or a housekeeper at a hotel, or a lunch-time hostess or barback in a busy theme restaurant, it's all the same.

But my heart lies with the waiters. I've had the pleasure to work with so many wonderful people in this business and the waiters were the best. I have been tough on them through the years, expecting much. But I've fought many fights behind the scenes to support them, to get them more equipment and better working conditions, to have them treated like the professionals they are. I have quietly won more fights on their behalf then they will ever know.

The waiters and bartenders are my backbone. Any good fortune I've received in this business would not have been possible without the efforts of countless people, people that have all worked very hard for me.

Remember: Being a waiter is an honorable job. Be proud of what you do. Stand tall, hold your head high. Treat your guests as you would treat your grandma. They will treat you well in return. **And maybe leave you a BIG tip…even if you're a bad waiter!**

~~~~~~~~~~~~~~~~~~~~~~~~~~

So it's time for you to leave? Sorry to see you go.

Well it's been my pleasure to take care of you today and it's great to see that you enjoyed your time as well.

Here's your coat, may I help you with your bags?

Oh, let me get the door for you and please watch your step.

Don't forget, my name is Steve and I hope to see you again soon! Please ask for me when you come back next time.

Goodnight and have a safe trip my friend.

…and remember, the book store you were interested in is a mile and a half up the road.

Author's Thanks

Thank you so much for purchasing this book. It was written out of my passion for customer service and to help my employees be the best they can…and hopefully earn BIGGER tips as well.

If you liked this book, please tell a friend about it and ask them to purchase it as well.

And if I can ask one more favor of you, **please go to Amazon.com and write a review about this book as well**. Amazon has turned into the world's largest book store and THE place to go when searching for a good read.

Your review will assist future readers to find this book and see for themselves the benefits of my "tips".

Thanks again and have a great day!

Steve DiGioia